RELENTLESSLY
PURSUED
by God

Events, People, and Circumstances
Divinely Choreographed by God for
My Appointed Time of Salvation

ROLAND F. ST. GERARD (BRORO)

WESTBOW
P R E S S®
A DIVISION OF THOMAS NELSON
& ZONDERVAN

WestBow Press books may be ordered through booksellers or by contacting:

WestBow Press
A Division of Thomas Nelson & Zondervan
1663 Liberty Drive
Bloomington, IN 47403
www.westbowpress.com
844-714-3454

Scripture marked (KJV) taken from the King James Version.

Scripture marked (NKJV) taken from the New King James Version®. Copyright © 1982 by Thomas Nelson. Used by permission. All rights reserved.

Scripture marked (WEB) taken from the World English Bible translation.

ISBN: 978-1-6642-0563-5 (sc)
ISBN: 978-1-6642-0565-9 (hc)
ISBN: 978-1-6642-0564-2 (e)

Library of Congress Control Number: 2020917604

Print information available on the last page.

WestBow Press rev. date: 10/02/2020

CONTENTS

CONTENTS

DOES GOD PURSUE PEOPLE FOR REAL?

God is looking for people to use, and if you can get usable, He will wear you out. The most dangerous prayer you can pray is this: "Use me."

—Rick Warren

Bible scriptures on the pursuit of God:

For the Son of Man came to seek and to save that which was lost.

—Luke 19:10 (WEB)

For the Lord Yahweh says: "Behold, I myself, even I, will search for my sheep, and will seek them out. As a shepherd seeks out his flock in the day that he is among his sheep that are scattered abroad, so I will seek out my sheep. I will deliver them out of all places where they have been scattered in the cloudy and dark day."

—Ezekiel 34:11–12 (WEB)

I have gone astray like a lost sheep. Seek your servant, for I don't forget your commandments.

—Psalm 119:176 (WEB)

I will seek that which was lost, and will bring back that which was driven away, and will bind up that which was broken, and will strengthen that which was sick; but I will destroy the fat and the strong. I will feed them in justice.

—Ezekiel 34:16 (WEB)

What do you think? If a man has one hundred sheep, and one of them goes astray, doesn't he leave the ninety-nine, go to the mountains, and seek that which has gone astray? If he finds it, most certainly I tell you, he rejoices over it more than over the ninety-nine which have not gone astray. Even so it is not the will of your Father who is in heaven that one of these little ones should perish.

—Matthew 18:12–14 (WEB)

But the hour comes, and now is, when the true worshipers will worship the Father in spirit and truth, for the Father seeks such to be his worshipers.

—John 4:23 (WEB)

SPECIAL NOTE: THE WORLD CAME TO A HALT

While I was writing the introduction to *Relentlessly Pursued by God*, the world had come to a halt. People all over the world began to experience a widespread crisis at the same time. While many people in the United States had in mind to prosper and fulfill their 20/20 vision of destiny this year, the news broke out that a virus that was more contagious than any other had hit the United States. I am referring to the coronavirus and the illness it causes. It has been officially called COVID-19. Governments of every nation began to give strict orders for their citizens to stay at home. Businesses were temporarily closed (some end up closing permanently), and parks, beaches, restaurants, sports arenas, and all other social gathering venues had to shut down. Whereas at first, people had the option of wearing masks; afterward, mask-wearing becomes law. Facemasks must be worn before entering stores, and everyone must maintain a distance of no less than six feet apart from each other. The majority of people could not go to work. Schools had to shut down and moved to online. Millions of people across the globe were hospitalized, and hundreds of thousands died. Due to the widespread nature of the contagion, expanding over a large geographical area; therefore, the World Health Organization (WHO) categorized it as a pandemic.

The pandemic, along with governmental initiatives, the constant updates by the media, various medical theories, and conspiracies, among other things, caused much panic and fear. Many people lost their jobs; some lost their businesses, and of course, many fell sick. Furthermore, experts in crisis intervention anticipate many mental disorders to arise amid this crisis due to job loss, financial burdens, grieving for loved ones, and the lack of face-to-face social connections.

The most prominent types of psychological distress people often show, are anxiety and fear. Psychologists have coined many kinds of strains that affect people mentally, such as free-floating anxiety, neurotic anxiety, moderate anxiety, intense anxiety, state anxiety, and trait anxiety. The list goes on. However, the stress that most people experience is "normal anxiety." According to Dr. Gary Collins (2007), *"Normal anxiety* comes to all of us at times, usually when there is some threat or situational danger. Most often, this anxiety is proportional to the danger: the greater the threat, the greater the anxiety, although sometimes we can't know how serious a threat may be. This is anxiety that can be recognized, managed, and reduced, especially when circumstances change and the danger is reduced" (141). From what the government, the media, and others are saying, the world will not be as we knew it before the pandemic, and therefore, we should anticipate living a new normal.

As a result of this "new normal," prayer becomes more needful. It's an odd phenomenon to see that in times of crisis, most people seem to be a bit more sluggish in their prayer lives. They get so engaged in watching the news, hearing other people's opinions, and wondering what's next that prayer becomes the last thing on their minds. But in Luke 18:1–8, Jesus told the disciples a story to help them realize that praying in and out of a crisis is crucial. Some individuals don't understand why people have to pray since God already knows their predicament. And the simple answer is that God has established a system whereby, although He knows what you are going through, someone still has to invite Him in that particular situation to intervene. Thus, we must pray!

In his book *Prayer Power*, Pastor Mosy Madugba explains that "Prayer is the act of communing with the Almighty God who created the heavens and the earth and all that live and exist in them. It is a link between the natural and the supernatural. It affords man, who is human, an opportunity to speak to God, who is Spirit. It enables the weak man to hook up to the most powerful being in existence and creates a channel through which the grace and the power of the supernatural God can flow into a natural man" (iv). In other words, just like you would not like to run to your children every time they encounter a challenge. Most parents would like to see the child make an effort to overcome the problem. If the situation becomes overbearing for the child, the child will cry or simply ask for help. Then Daddy and mommy will run to the rescue. God operates similarly. He prefers that we attempt to solve our difficulties with the abilities that He has gifted us with, with the help of the Holy Spirit. And if the situation seems too much to bear, we or someone else have to call on Him for help. The power of God is available for all who call upon Him with all their hearts. The apostle Paul encourages the Philippians not to worry about anything but to pray about everything.

As human beings, we are more prone to worry when facing some form of danger, threat, or uncertainties than to count on the power and faithfulness of Almighty God. However, the fact is, no matter what you are going through, no matter the challenge or difficulty, you are not alone. God is with you and even in you. The Lord Jesus promises that He will always be with you and never leave you. The Bible tells us that Jesus is the truth, and therefore cannot lie. In that case, believe it; He is waiting to hear from you in prayer. God promises to show you incredible things when you look for Him with all your heart. So, no matter how you feel, whether it's fear, anxiety, or grief, you must pray. For, when you invite God into the situation, you give Him the legal right to show up in your particular predicament and set His peace as a shield to guard your heart and to protect you from a nervous breakdown or the worse.

I urge you to call on God while in your fragile state, and you will find yourself to be strong enough, bold enough, and courageous enough not only to pray for yourself and your family but also to pray for others. You will acquire the power to pray for your neighbors, your church family, the persecuted church, and your leaders. The peace of God within you will help you to pray for government leaders, church leaders, community leaders, your employer, and for all who are in an authoritative position. Praying for all leaders is a noble task for all followers of Jesus Christ. The apostle Paul declares, "I *urge*, that, first of all, supplications, prayers, intercessions, and giving of thanks, be made for all men; For kings, and for all that are in authority; that we may lead a quiet and peaceable life in all godliness and honesty. For this is good and acceptable in the sight of God our Saviour" (1 Timothy 2:1-3 KJV). When you call on the Lord, even in your painful moments, you will find yourself transformed from a prayerless worrier to a prayerful warrior.

Even though we can't be sure of what tomorrow holds, if we know who holds tomorrow, we will not worry about tomorrow. The apostle Paul states that when you go to God in prayer instead of worrying, and when you give Him praise for receiving your answered prayer by faith, God's peace will protect your heart and your mind. That means you will feel whole and complete—nothing missing, nothing lacking, even amid adverse circumstances. Paul encouraged the Philippians, saying, "Don't worry about anything; instead, pray about everything. Tell God what you need, and thank him for all he has done. Then you will experience God's peace, which exceeds anything we can understand. His peace will guard your hearts and minds as you live in Christ Jesus" (Philippians 4:6-7 NLT).

In these unprecedented moments, securing your trust in the Lord Jesus should be your foremost priority. Hours His crucifixion, Jesus told the disciples, "Peace I leave with you, My peace I give unto you: not as the world giveth, give I unto you. Let not your heart be troubled; neither let it be afraid" (John 14:27 KJV). These remarkable promises of God ought to inspire you to become a great prayer warrior and lead you to begin to pray confidently, meditate upon God's Word deeply, and declare God's promises unapologetically.

One simple way you can begin to pray when you don't feel like praying is to start with gratitude. Begin by thanking God for the apparent blessings you have enjoyed and are now enjoying in life. For example, if you can see, if you can hear, if you can taste, If you can move about, you have food to eat; if you can move your fingers, if you can walk and touch, and most of all if you can breathe, you can begin to give thanks for each one of these abilities. While one person with hearing abilities might not be able to see, and some can touch but can't feel, each one of us, in particular, has something that someone else might not have. So, if you take a minute and reflect, you will find that no matter what you are going through, you have more than enough reasons to be grateful.

There are significant psychological and spiritual benefits of expressing gratitude. In an in-depth study done in 2013 on the psychology of gratitude with fifty-one participants ranging in age from eighteen to eighty, the participants identified particular emotions in response to being grateful: "feelings such as sensations in [the] heart and chest, joy, release, acceptance/comfort/security, love, warmth, blessed, awakening, awe, presence, thankful, etc." (Elfers and Hlava 2016, 31). The positive effects of gratitude are real. You might be feeling like this is the end of the world for you. Still, if you dare begin to thank God for everything in your life, small and significant accomplishments, you will start to feel much better. That feeling will lead to a more hopeful and productive lifestyle, even amid a pandemic.

While some people will make it through prayer and the studying of God's word, the stark reality is, some folks will require expert support to deal with fear and anxiety. Some God-fearing individuals might need to see a Christian counselor, that is someone who is licensed in the psychological field and, at the same time, is a sincere believer in the Lord Jesus Christ. Dr. Collins defines a Christian counselor as "a deeply committed, Spirit-guided (and Spirit-filled) servant of Jesus Christ. Who applies his or her God-given abilities, skills, training, knowledge, and insights to the task of helping others move to personal wholeness, interpersonal competence, mental stability, and spiritual maturity" (Collins 2001, 21). We thank God for the Holy Spirit, for the Word of God, and Christian fellowship. Still, sometimes our situation requires a believer who is trained as a professional counselor to help us understand what we're going through and how to transition from being hurtful to be helpful.

One of the reasons for seeking professional help from a Christian counselor is that we are tripartite beings. We are spirit, soul, and body. Through our spiritual nature, we connect to God. However, we use our bodies, through our mouths and gestures, to do the verbal praying and praise expressions. Therefore, since we have particular psychological traits, mindsets, and traumatic experiences, there are times when a specialist in the mental field who, at the same time, understands what it is to have faith in Christ is needed to help get us through some overwhelming situations.

Some Christians don't think believers should seek psychological counsel. Part of their argument is that God and the Bible are enough; we don't need anything else. In that case, we would not need to seek medical help or even exercise for our physical well-being. On a spiritual plane, we have the Bible, the Holy Spirit, and our prayers and worship of God, through Jesus Christ, for our spiritual well-being. On the intellect level, we must maintain our mental well-being by reading, meditating, and living a balanced life of soul care. Notwithstanding that, when situations challenge us beyond our mental capacity, when we have prayed or tried to pray and have stood in faith, and still feel like giving up on life, then seeking help from the proper experts is advised.

The apostle Paul, a competent scholar and one who deeply loved the Lord, who committed his whole life to serve Master Jesus, prayed a prayer of wholeness for the Thessalonian believers. He prayed that "the very God of peace sanctify you wholly, and I pray God your whole spirit and soul and body be preserved blameless unto the coming of our Lord Jesus Christ" (1 Thessalonians 5:23 KJV). Paul understood that each part of the three aspects of humans needs particular care.

That is why I encourage you, that if fear and anxiety are affecting you or anyone you know because of COVID-19 or any other reason, remember you can pray. Furthermore, remember to give God thanks for the apparent blessings in your life. And if need be, please seek a Christian counselor who can help you put things in the proper perspective so that you can live the abundant life of Jesus even during the global pandemic.

While writing the introduction to *Relentlessly Pursued by God*, I felt that I should encourage you, the fact that we are now entered a new way of life.

Be blessed, and may you enjoy reading about how God pursues people for their deliverance.

INTRODUCTION

You can only understand properly if your
concepts are in alignment with your ideas,
and your ideas must be based upon God's
dynamic truth.

—Myles Munroe

What a paradox? As I was working in the nightclub years
ago before knowing Jesus as my personal Lord and Savior,
I often would take a reflective moment right before the
party crowd began to arrive. As I stood in the parking lot,
I got to delight in the "Compas" sound that was thumping
through the walls of the church. The people in the church
were having a great time singing, dancing, and yet without
anyone getting drunk.

Psalm 150:1–6 (WEB) urges everyone breathing to praise
the Lord:

Praise Yah! Praise God in His sanctuary!
Praise Him in the heavens for His acts of power.
Praise Him for His mighty acts! Praise Him according to His excellent greatness!
Praise Him with the sounding of the trumpet!
Praise Him with harp and lyre!
Praise Him with the tambourine and dancing!
Praise Him with loud cymbals!
Let everything that has breath praise the Yah!
Praise Yah!

I began to think and acknowledged to myself the fact that these joyful Christians were in their world, and I was in mine. Their world included going to church, and my world was the nightclub. Their world included praying. My world, drinking beer and whiskey. Their world included fellowshipping with one another for the glory of God. My world was to hook up with a girl for the night. I understood they were Christians, and I was not. And I respected the different worlds. But I never thought that I would ever become one of them, to the point of being a minister of the Gospel of Jesus Christ.

I did not grow up in the church. But I did use to go to the Catholic church in my town to ring the bell. Since the church was always open, and the priests were not around,

I went in and started to pull on those heavy ropes and ring the big bells. Those bells were supposed to ring at particular times, such as noontime and six o'clock. But as a little boy, I did not think of who could hear the bells ring. I figured it was a fun thing to do. And that was my church experience.

Eventually, after enjoying the joyful sound that was coming from the church outside, it was time now for me to go inside the club to begin setting the atmosphere for exuberant partying. My job was to make sure that the customers have a spectacular time musical wise. The challenge was that every department in the club depended on how the music would play out. The owners expected to make money at the door with the admission fee. Money had to be made with the food that was available for sale. But the primary money machine was the bars serving beer, whiskey, and other drinks stationed upfront and toward the back of the club. Unless the music went well, it would hurt these other departments of the club.

Although I was the star DJ of the club, I did not have many friends, though. Neither did I like being the center of attention. I often refrained from approaching people whom I did not know. But that did not stop me from getting on the dance floor on my break time when a lively beat was playing. And I did not mind dancing all by myself as if I was putting a show. However, the moment I thought people were looking at me dancing, it did fuel my motivation to put on a show. There was this one time when I felt moved to step out of my shell and mustered up some boldness to ask a woman to dance. Being afraid of rejection, I had to find a skillful way to approach to communicate my request. As if it was by inspiration, I slid close to her and said, "Would it be a crime if I asked you to dance with me?" She simply smiled and followed me to the dance floor.

My daytime was a bit different from the night scene. I got to socialize with a few friends of mine. Thus, my average weekday consisted of visiting a couple of acquaintances. I would visit my Jamaican friend to drink carrot juice, talk about future reggae events, and relax in his wooden gated backyard. These friends were older than I was, and they were family men. My friend, whose house I visited, was a music producer and artist management. He produced the work of reggae artists from Jamaica. But, it just so happened that God used this particular friend to direct me to watch Christian television, which was one of the tools God used in his pursue to prepare my heart for salvation.

Besides that, I witnessed a couple of voodoo ceremonies when I was a little boy. The first one happened in my younger childhood years. There was a family who hosted a big feast to the spirits on behalf of their twin children. They decorated a long table filled with all sorts of goodies.

There was cake, candy, fruits, and vegetables, and they had adorned the place with beautiful, lively colors. I was pretty young when I witnessed that ceremony. I even ate some of the food from the table.

When I got a bit older, I observed another voodoo ceremony. I did not have a thorough knowledge of the tradition and the activities, but I guess I was intrigued by the songs, the drum, and the participants' confident outlook while engaged in that service. Since I was not a Christian and did not grow up in church, I regarded these events as regular cultural events, like throwing a party, which people tend to do. Overall, I did not identify with any particular religion, although my family professed the Catholic faith.

If the Lord had not pursued me when He did, I would still be out in the world as a DJ, an artist, or something worse. Look what God has done! I am now a dynamic and anointed preacher, a life coach, and a writer. I preach and teach the whole counsel of the Word of God to help instill a thorough comprehension of the revealed mysteries of the kingdom of God. I conduct live and online conferences and workshops on prayer, faith, mind renewal (what some refer to as "kingdom paradigm"), and the Christian lifestyle.

When I encounter some of my former friends, fans, and foes, their reaction is, "If God can save you, then He can save me too." In hearing those words, on the one hand, I rejoice, knowing that God can use my life as an example of what He's willing to do for others. On the other hand, it makes me wonder about how naughty I must have been. Their remarks cause me to think back to determine what I was doing that was so awful. And they were right: I was terrible. I used to cuss, smoke, drink, sleep with countless women, and live an aimless life as if I was a vagabond.

Maybe this is not a story "From rags to riches?" But, where I came from spiritually, socially, and even materially to get to where I am today as a preacher, teacher, life coach, and author, you might as well say I have been resurrected by the resurrection power of the Lord Jesus Christ.

Let us now enter the story!

RELENTLESSLY PURSUED BY GOD

They did not see that coming. I got to the radio station, where for the past months, I had been the one controlling the board to open the six-hour daily radio program and to put other presenters on the air. When I got to the radio station on that rainy day in the beautiful sunshine state, the staff got the news they never thought they would have heard from me in a thousand years. I told the on-site manager and others that were present that, I would not be playing secular music (Compas, reggae, calypso) any longer but only Christian music, because I have accepted Jesus as my Savior. That was a shocker. What? Cool C, playing only Christian music? That's unheard of.

Working with owners and the staff of that community radio program was a great privilege. At that time, I only had a high school level education, and both the managers and presenters were the public intellectuals of the community at that time. I appreciated the fact that the president of the company and others gave me that opportunity. In my then world, it was a prestigious position. However, my God came for me. And the greatest prestige is that which is found in answering the call of the Creator and King of the universe.

However, since I used to smoke marijuana, some of the staff and others thought, I might have gone crazy. Maybe I did too much of the smoking. So now I have gone religious on them. My colleagues could not believe it, my night club friends and fans could not either, and those who listen to me on the radio went into a shock. Because, since I was an on-air person, my conversion was a public event, although, as you will discover, it was first a very private matter between God and me.

Almost three decades later, I am now still being kept by the grace and faithfulness of God. I continue to share Christ with the lost and teach believers the word of God. Moreover, ministering the Gospel of the Lord Jesus Christ to help foster transformation in others is firstly beneficial for me. For, as a preacher, I get to prepare sermons just about every week. It is unquestionably more desirous than the prestige I had enjoyed in the world. With this new relationship with the Lord Jesus and walking in the vocation to which He called me, I get to preach at various churches, share principles of God's kingdom on the radio. I teach biblical truths at conferences and revival services. This line of work demands that I research multiple books and other external informative sources for adequate preparation. Ultimately, I get to rejoice greatly, seeing how my preaching and teaching significantly impact people's lives. It is eternally gratifying.

My earliest memory of the events of my life goes back to my toddler years. From there, life seemed to have begun to scurry for me. I started to get drunk as a young boy, experienced sexual activities by my initiation, and, in my older years as a teenager and young adult, I experienced marijuana smoking.

Relentlessly Pursued by God is the story of the pursuit of God that transformed a drunken, purposeless boy growing up on the backside of a little town in northwest Haiti to have become now a pastor, preacher, and life-changer in the United States. You will follow the pursuit from my baby years through the developmental years, to the life and destiny threatening years, until we reached to where the chase ended. Then, again, to begin a new lease in life with a better perspective.

I have seen it in the movies. I have heard people tell stories about it; angelic visitations. It was the most unparalleled experience I have gone through. It was three o'clock in the morning. I knew the time because whenever I wake up in the middle of the night, the first thing I do is to see what time it is. I sat up in bed, and, as I looked toward the foot of the be, I saw a person about six feet standing there. We did not enter into any conversation. Only that, the moment I sighted him, he quickly announced a Bible verse to me. After hearing the announcement, I immediately jumped out of bed to go look up the verse in the Bible. After he gave the message, he was gone. After reading the passage, I found myself following the leading of the Spirit of God. I went straight to the corner of the room, diagonal to the bed, about two feet away, I knelt and prayed. It was there during that prayer session that Father God communicated His heart to me.

THE BEGINNING OF
MY PREDICAMENT

THE DRUNKEN BOY

I was no older than four or five years of age when my mother left my two siblings and me in Haiti to forge a new life in the United States. We did not have any father(s) to raise us or discipline us. My mother left us with an older woman who did her best to watch over us with the help of neighbors and other acquaintances of my mother. As a result, we children found ourselves moved from one house to another.

But when she left, we were living in a large house that divides into two to three-family occupancies—occupied by two or three families. While growing up in that part of the town, I got to experience things that most children have no business experiencing. I got to experience both drunkenness and sexual activity very early in life. In those years, there was a carpentry shop positioned directly across the street from where I lived. There was also a little house in the same small lot of the carpentry shop. I spent my days at the shop touching things, talking to the men, and playing around as if I were one of the workers. The men met there daily to build furniture, coffins, and other woodwork. But they took the day off on Sundays.

Even though the men didn't work on Sundays, they still met at the shop. They got together to play dominoes and cards and drink hard liquor. As they played their games, drank, smoked, and joked around, I was there drinking as well. Back in the '70s, no law in Haiti prohibited adults from giving children liquor to drink. I was six years old, when, after drinking some whiskey, I went off running up and down the dirt road, riding on a broomstick as if I was on a horse.

One of the funniest and horrible episodes of my drunkenness was when I imitated the "Mardi Gras Lance" members. Those are a group of roots band members that decorated their bodies, from head to toe with mud. They followed a particular path with changing and a type of lasso (lance) to lasso specific people. I don't have thorough information about their full representation. However, on one of those golden days, I also decorated myself with mud from head to toe, and around town.

Alcohol-drinking negatively affects millions of Americans over the years. Furthermore, alcohol can be extremely damaging to people's lives in many ways. I thank God for His grace and for keeping me from being damaged from those moments of intoxication. Alcohol has caused much loss of life. According to the National Center for Biotechnology Information (NCBI), "Alcohol is the most common drug used among adults in the United States. The use of alcohol is associated with an increased risk of injuries and accidents. Even a single episode of excessive drinking can lead to a negative outcome. Alcoholism and chronic use of alcohol are associated with numerous medical, psychiatric, social, and family problems."[1] Moreover, the World Health Organization (WHO) reports, "Every year the harmful use of alcohol is estimated to kill 2.5 million people, of whom 320,000 are young people aged between 15 and 29 years. Alcohol is implicated in one-quarter of all homicides globally. Studies linking youth violence and harmful alcohol use have been conducted in several countries."[2]

People drink for various reasons. Some people drink to drown away their troubles, some for relaxation, and some drink by habit, something they picked up along the way. Others inherit the practice. It is hereditary. Some people's drinking practice is bound up in a spiritual contract in which their family is engaged. We often see the marks of these spiritual contracts on families. These marks manifest in terms of promiscuity, futility, alcoholism, and others. The members who engaged or are aware of these agreements continue to pay homage to particular spirits as a duty. When people finally receive Jesus as their personal Lord and Savior, spiritually, they enter into a new blood covenant (agreement). The blood of Jesus Christ cleanses them from the old spiritual bloodline, .and is given a new spiritual DNA. In my ancient spiritual bloodline, I was a foolish attraction in my childhood years because of my drunkenness. However, my alliance with Jesus Christ has made me a new attraction—God embellishes me with the radiance of His glory. I don't get drunk on whiskey and beer any longer. I now get drunk in the Holy Spirit. The Apostle Paul told the Christians in Ephesus, "Don't be drunken with wine, in which is dissipation, but be filled with the Spirit; singing, and making melody in your heart to the Lord" (Eph. 5:18-19, WEB).

When the Holy Spirit came down like a mighty rushing wind on the Day of Pentecost in Jerusalem, fifty days after the resurrection of the Lord Jesus, the disciples were full of the wine of the Spirit. They were drunk with the goodness, the power, and the revelation of God. Jews who were visiting Jerusalem from various parts of the world observed that the disciples reacted blissfully and spoke in different languages. Some of them thought the disciples were drunk. Peter, therefore, stood up and clarified things for them. He explained that these people were not drunk as some thought but that they were observing the fulfillment of the promise that God had made a long time ago. He made this promise through His prophet Joel—that in the last days, He would pour His Spirit upon all flesh, which would enable them to prophesy, dream dreams, and work wonders.

I believe that as you follow the story of how God relentlessly pursued me to bring lasting transformation to my heart from drunkenness to holiness, you too will be touched by the power of the Holy Spirit. As you continue to read, anticipate a special touch by the Holy Spirit that will elevate your spiritual experience to a new dimension.

SEXUAL EXPERIENCE AS A TODDLER

Drunkenness was not the only vice that had a hold on my life. I had a subjective sexual event as an infant. I was mindful enough to remember what led to the incident but not the actual development. One of the adults in the house asked a teenage girl who was part of the household to feed me a bowl of soup. She must have been hungry or liked the look and the smell of the soup because she started to eat of the soup more than feeding me. Realizing that, I revolted. And she immediately whispered something in my ear. After she whispered to me in my ear what is now a mystery to me, I let her have the soup. Then, when night fell, and everybody went to sleep, she took me next door to the neighbors' storage room located at the back of the house next door. I have no idea what happened in that storage room that night. When morning came around, someone came and discovered us fully naked. I do have some doubts, however, of the particular activities that transpired that night.

Even though a sensual and physical activity might have taken place, it is also probable that some destiny foul-play occurred that night. The kingdom of darkness is deceitful and uses people of all ages to recruit and interfere in spiritually gullible individuals. They utilize whatever means necessary to accomplish their plans, such as using magic, jinx, fetish, and various means to intrude in other people's souls. Since God knows what transpired that night and for what purpose and nothing goes unnoticed to my Maker, His pursuit of me also involved the reversing of all evil spiritual manipulation of my destiny.

Retrospectively, I see the Lord, like in the days of Moses, when He came down in the burning bush to call Moses out of the wilderness to deliver the Israelites from slavery, so He had done for me as well. God told Moses, "I have surely seen the affliction of my people which are in Egypt, and have heard their cry because of their taskmasters; for I know their sorrows, and I am come down to deliver them out the hand of the Egyptians" (Exodus 3:7–8a KJV). Similarly, I believe that if that young lady did anything of evil spiritual nature to impede my life in any way, undoubtedly, the Lord has overturned it. I trust that the Lord has rendered it ineffective. When God saw my life was spiraling downward to oblivion, He set to rescue me by pursuing me by all means until I would come to the point of recognizing Jesus Christ as my personal Lord and Savior.

MY FIRST VOLUNTARY SEXUAL ENCOUNTER AT AGE SEVEN

When I was a toddler, the teenage girl did to me as she pleased, and I was not even mindful of what she did. When I was in my childhood years, it was another story. I was seven years old, and I was sent to the store one day by an adult living in the house in which I lived. On my way to the store, I spotted my playmate, who was a girl my age. She was standing in front of her mother's porch across the street. She noticed that I was eating a peanut bar, and decided to ask me to give her a piece. The road separated us.

She was standing at a distance of about fifty feet away from me. So when she asked me to give her a piece of my bar, I impulsively told her, "I will give you a piece only if we spend some time together when I return." She quickly agreed, and I rushed to the store and hurried back. After giving the adult the item I was sent to buy, I promptly walked across the street to keep my promise of given my friend girl a piece of the peanut bar. From there, we instantly engaged in sexual contact.

Her mom had gone to the market. In the interim of passionate kiddy romance, I sometimes stopped to look outside to check if her mom was coming. I went outside three or four times. Each time, I stepped out and glanced both ways, all the while, not knowing that the adults were sitting across the street, outside the house where I lived, watching my ins and outs. Soon afterward, one of the adults sent someone to call me over. When I obediently went to her, she inspected my private part and affirmed that what she had suspected was accurate. So by a measure of discipline, she ordered me to kneel in the backyard, which was full of cracked dried mud. There was no grass in the yard, only dirt, mostly mud during the raining season.

According to my recollection, my sexual activities did not resume until I was about twelve years old after coming to the United States. My teenage and young adult years ushered in a lifestyle of promiscuity. I did not keep a steady girlfriend; therefore, I was free to engage with as many as was available. For some people, this lifestyle is beyond fleshly desires. For most non-Christians, having sex with multiple women and outside of marriage is somewhat the norm. However, the spiritual-minded person understands that the spirit world influences many of our sensual human activities. As a result, finding oneself engaged naturally in illicit sex is, for the most part, something inherited by ancestral spiritual alliances. Many people enter into spiritual contracts with all sorts of spirits for protection, prominence, or power. These contracts, depending on the conditions set, affect the descendants of the contract signer.

The Bible tells us that "Yahweh is slow to anger, and abundant in loving kindness, forgiving iniquity and disobedience; and that will by no means clear the guilty, visiting the iniquity of the fathers on the children, on the third and on the fourth generation" (Numbers 14:18 WEB). Visiting the iniquities of the subsequent generations means that whatever sin, evil, or demonic contract our ancestors had entered into three or four generations prior still is binding on the current generation and beyond. As mentioned before, if you take note of the lifestyles of particular families, you will notice some apparent marks of negative spiritual influences in the lives of the members of these families. You might observe that some of the members engage in multi-partner relationships, some are entrenched in drinking, others in witchcraft, poverty, and other such manifestations. It does not mean that every poor person is affected by such influence. But for the most part, if you would trace their family lines, you will most likely find that there is a spiritual connection somewhere that is influencing the ancestry line of that person.

Notice the questions asked when filling out a medical form. Most of the questions asked are about your family's medical background. They want to know whether any members of your family have suffered from heart conditions, high blood pressure, diabetes, and so on, which would indicate certain negative traits that may be present in your body. If you answer yes to any such questions, the doctors classify you as a candidate for such sickness or disease because it follows your family line.

It is apparent then, how I got into sexual activities at such a young age? No one trained me. It was in my bloodline. And the spirit of disobedience and rebellion was governing my life in that context. Paul told the Ephesians that before coming to Christ, they had walked according to the ways of this world. They walked according to the spirits that are controlling the air. These spirits are now working in people who are disobedient to God, driving them to act according to the desires of their carnal nature (Eph. 2). These spirits' tasks are similar to the law system in a country. The same way the court system and law enforcement are there to enforce contracts that are signed in this natural world, so it is with the spirit world. The spirits are employed to ensure that individuals and the members of their family follow the destructive lifestyle pattern of sex, alcohol, drugs, and the like. The apostle Paul teaches that we are in a fight and that it is not a physical one where we fight human beings, but a spiritual battle. "For we wrestle not against flesh and blood, but principalities, against powers, against the rulers of the darkness of this world, against spiritual wickedness in high places" (Eph. 6:12, KJV). These spirits are of various categories to enforce and reinforce the mandates of the kingdom of darkness and its evil activities. According to Dr. Tony Evans, "Behind every physical disturbance, setback, ailment, or issue we face lies a spiritual root. Unless we first identify and deal with the root spiritual cause, our attempts to fix the physical problem will provide only temporary relief at best. In other words, everything that your five senses experience physically is first generated by something that your five senses cannot detect" (2011, 14).

As a child of God, you can stand on God's curse-breaking Word by faith and declare, "Thanks be to God, who gives us the victory through our Lord Jesus Christ" (1 Cor. 15:57

WEB), "I am free." The Lord Jesus Christ redeemed us from every curse. We were set free from all evil and destructive ancestral contracts in the mighty name of Jesus Christ! Amen! Paul explained to the Galatians in the third chapter that "Christ redeemed, us, rescued us, liberated us from the curse."

Imagine having your first sexual encounter as a toddler, then beginning to get drunk as a young boy. That's what I did. Then, soon after, I was led to smoking cigarettes.

THE EFFECTS OF NICOTINE

My siblings and I were like pilgrims, moving from one house to another. Before long, the older woman who was our guardian moved to a new home close to the center of town in a closed-up community with a paved yard on which sat three or four houses. During the day, she went off visiting friends on the outskirts of town and in the hills. Sometimes she took me along, but most times, she left us at another woman's house to spend the day until evening time, when she returned. Soon after, as she became well advanced in age and felt that she could no longer carry on that responsibility, she took my two siblings and me to live at a relative's house. After dropping us off there, she went her way, never to return.

That was a house that was already full of other relatives living there. It was evident that the three of us made the house overcrowded. Naturally, this period of my life served more as a character-building and training ground to accelerate my maturity.

While there, at the age of eight years old, a family member frequently sent me to the little house store across the street to buy cigarettes—not a pack, but one or two sticks of cigarettes. Most of the time, after purchasing the cigarettes, I also had to light it up for her. Logically, one cannot light up a cigarette without inhaling it to trigger the spark. However, after having done that often enough, the power of nicotine hooked me and thrust me into smoking addiction.

It was easy to buy and light up a cigarette for the adult family member, but if I wanted to buy it for myself, it would have been disobedient. So, I could not be so bold to buy one for myself; neither did I have the money to do so. But because I had to light up the cigarette and inhale the tobacco smoke so many times, I became a smoker at the age of eight. And since I could not buy my own cigarettes, I did the next most natural thing I could do: I looked around for cigarette butts that adults had smoked and thrown away. When I found them, I hid far away to smoke.

The catch-22 of inhaling cigarette smoke is the damaging effect of the power of nicotine on the brain and the lungs; it is a dominant drug that enslaves most people who dare to try it once or twice. There are plenty of publications on the effects of nicotine on the human brain and the lungs. According to the Mayo Clinic, "Nicotine dependence—also called tobacco dependence—is an addiction to tobacco products caused by the drug nicotine. Nicotine dependence means you can't stop using the substance, even though it's causing you harm. Nicotine produces physical and mood-altering effects in your brain that are temporarily pleasing. These effects make you want to use tobacco and lead to dependence. At the same time, stopping tobacco use causes withdrawal symptoms, including irritability and anxiety."[3]

Because of the power of nicotine, I struggled for many years trying to quit smoking. I had thrown packs of cigarettes away, claiming that I would no longer smoke cigarettes. But it did not take long before I returned to the store to purchase more. I was trapped. The stronghold of cigarettes had gripped me; I was under the control of nicotine. But thank God for the power that is greater than all earthly and heavenly powers that finally came to my rescue. The power of God's love through the shed blood of Jesus Christ astonishingly broke the dominance of nicotine in my life, even though that breakthrough took me by surprise.

One day, in my young adult years, while visiting a friend of mine, I stood on the inside of his wooden-gated backyard. In an unplanned act, but being tired of being overtly defeated by nicotine, I pulled out a cigarette and started to talk to it. I didn't have any second thoughts about it. I was not thinking of who could be watching me talk to a seemingly lifeless object. But I stood there by the gate inside my friend's yard before knocking at his house door. I spoke to the cigarette and said, "Look how small and short and lifeless you are, and look how big I am. Yet I have been allowing you to rule my life for so long. Therefore, if I ever I smoke you again, you will be the champion and I the loser." Since that declaration in October 1992, I have never picked up a cigarette to smoke, and neither have I entertained the desire to smoke ever again. That did not stop the spirits from offering me the chance to smoke in my dreams. I have seen myself with cigarettes two or three times in my night dreams. Even so, the Lord has set me free totally and forever.

MY EXPERIENCE WITH MARIJUANA

You would think sex, alcohol, and cigarettes would be sufficient enough for this restless soul. But it seemed that I had another rung on the substance abuse ladder to climb.

What a life! I was no stranger to doing as a child and a teenager what adults do—although it was still wrong for anyone at any age to do. After I came to the United States in 1978 to reunite with my mother in Miami, Florida, I began to adapt to the way of life. That would not come without its tests and challenges. After rejoining my mother at the age of twelve, I also got to meet my little brother, along with my little cousin. They both were born in the United States. At that time, we lived in Little Haiti. Both the parents lived in separate units in the same triplex apartment. The two of them—my brother and my cousin—had grown up together like two brothers. They are about seven years younger than I am.

Due to inferiority complexity, I felt out of place when I could not understand them when they talked. As a result, I got frustrated at times. In other words, I felt like I did not belong. For a brief moment, I had the "going back to Haiti" syndrome. One of the ways this syndrome is evident is when a person who has recently come from Haiti feels rejected or mistreated by another family member. That feeling generates a strong urge to go back to Haiti. It was something like when the Israelites were set free from slavery in Egypt. Every time they faced a challenge, they wanted to go back to Egypt. Not that I am comparing Haiti with enslavement. Haiti is a beautiful paradise, without the chaotic political turmoil that is ravaging the land. Thus, that is one of the ways the going-back-to-Haiti syndrome manifests. Hence, when the two of them interacted with one another in English while I could not understand, I thought my brother and my cousin were talking negatively about me and did not want me around. As a result, I felt terrible and just wanted to go back to my country. Lol.

The syndrome is also noticeable when a parent or family member helps bring a child, a brother, a sister, or someone else from Haiti to the United States. When the host family member feels as if the sponsored member is somehow disrespecting him or her or standing in opposition, the host usually threatens to send that family member back to Haiti. My case, however, was the former; I had the "going back to Haiti" syndrome. But that was quickly fixed by the intervention of my mother, along with my aunt. They resolved the communication gap between the boys and me, and then I became an official member of the partnership for that season. As a member of the English-speaking brothers, my English skills began to accelerate to keep up with my new playing buddies. Indeed, particular children's television programs helped with my English comprehension training.

Soon enough, we moved from midtown to a place a few miles north in the same city. Then we moved once again before my mother and stepfather (deceased) were able to buy a nice-size house, in which my mother lived from 1979 to summer 2019 when she passed away. I lived there on and off until I accepted the Lord Jesus as my Savior. Remarkably, it was there I received the heavenly visitation that led me to the decision of recognizing and accepting Jesus as my Savior.

I made some great friends growing up in that neighborhood. This group of friends was mostly boys, but there were a few girls too. We occasionally went to the park together to play basketball. Sometimes we played football on the street by the house. At other times, we attended parties in the neighborhood. There was some minor attraction between some of the members, but no significant relationships ensued. I had never seen any of these friends either smoke or drink.

I was the one who had the bad habits of drinking, smoking, and being promiscuous. It so happened that I met an individual who was not a part of this group of friends. I got to experience marijuana for the first time. We started smoking. After taking a few puffs, I began to feel like I was in the air. Then we decided to walk to the nearby fast-food restaurant, which was eight blocks away. It was about 8:30 in the evening. After walking for a couple of blocks, we suddenly took off running. We ran to the restaurant nonstop. As we got to the restaurant, we saw people standing in line, ordering, and waiting for their food. However, the most thrilling part of the scene was that a police officer was also standing there. I instinctively began to panic on the inside, but I managed to keep my cool on the outside.

Nicotine has a particular effect on people's health. Marijuana, on the other hand, affects people in varying degrees, depending on several factors. The length of time a person has been a smoker and the amount he or she smoked, along with the individual's psychological makeup, determine the level of effects. All these factors account for how marijuana affects a person who smokes.

The Centers for Disease Control and Prevention (CDC) explains, "Marijuana use directly affects the brain—specifically the parts of the brain responsible for memory, learning, attention, decision-making, coordination, emotions, and reaction. ... Marijuana also affects brain development. When marijuana users begin using it as teenagers, the drug may reduce attention, memory, and learning functions, and affect how the brain builds connections between the areas necessary for these functions."[4]

The misuse and abuse of marijuana end up affecting the brain in ways that are damaging to the person's well-being.

Undeniably, God's power and grace preserved me that these substances did not hurt my reasoning capabilities.

MY STORY OF COCAINE USE

The question now was, would I go higher on the drug chain? Alcohol, tobacco, marijuana—could I do any worse than that? There is an exceptional mystery in the providential acts of God that some people would oppose. Even though it was not God who led me to use these addictive substances, I am almost sure that He was involved in preventing me from moving on to more potent drugs that would ultimately destroy me. Perfect example: A young man I met at the last elementary grade level took me for a visit one evening to a place in one of the roughest parts of town. As we entered the small apartment through the living room with a little kitchen table adjacent to the kitchen, I saw there was some white powdery substance on the table. Before he and the resident of the apartment went into the bedroom to talk, he told me to help myself to the cocaine abundantly lined up on the table. This friend has subsequently passed away.

After we graduated from elementary school, he and I lost touch for an extended time. Then, mysteriously, toward the end of my eleventh-grade school year, I began to contemplate how I was a bit too old to be in high school. As I was in deep reflection about being too old to be in school, my friend from the past resurfaced. It was almost like he appeared out of nowhere. But this time he had a car. He also had a job. So, after work, he would pick me up to drive around, doing nothing serious but merely hanging out. We drove around town drinking and smoking.

And there I was, years later, after our first meeting in elementary school, standing in this apartment with a table arrayed with rows of cocaine, offered to me freely, at no cost. Mind you; people paid a lot of money for things like that in those days. Being offered such a drug at no price is in no way the same thing as when Jesus, in Isaiah 55, called out to everybody who desired to come and eat, "Buy milk and wine with no money, without cost."

"Take as much as you'd like," my friend said to me. Thank God that I had enough intuitive sense, and also a fear of that substance, to say no. I just imagined how this substance would take full control of my brain and paralyze my life or simply kill me.

It is not surprising, the path my life took given that I'd come from a lineage of people who served ancestral spirits throughout many generations. The lifestyle of sex, drugs, and alcohol I so quickly engaged in at such a young age!

All those things are manifestations of the unseen spirits in the hidden world.

Dr. D. K. Olukoya sheds some light on this spiritual concept in his book *Prayer Rain*. He writes:

> In architecture, the foundation is the most important part of a building. This is the part on which the whole building will rest. It must be solid. The height of the building is determined by the foundation.
>
> Where we get in life depends on the kind of foundation we have. The ability to read is the foundation for further education. It is impossible for an illiterate to graduate from a university.
>
> Many of us have foundations that will limit and hinder our physical and spiritual progress. Such foundations are the result of evil dedications and evil inheritance, which have now become bondage, limiting your success in life. The enemy of man's soul knows how to convert footholds to strongholds. The good news is that as a believer, a born again, spirit-filled Christian, our foundation is Christ.[5]

The path that my life followed was not an uncommon one given the ancestral spiritual foundation that was laid for me by the previous generations. Paul told the Ephesians, "You were made alive when you were dead in transgressions and sins, in which you once walked according to the course of this world, according to the prince of the power of the air, the spirit who now works in the children of disobedience. We also all once lived among them in the lusts of our flesh, doing the desires of the flesh and of the mind, and were by nature children of wrath, even as the rest" (Ephesians 2:1–4 WEB).

We naturally inherit a distorted foundation because of the fallen nature of Adam, and our ancestors reinforce it by individual spiritual acts that they perform. It is clear from Paul's stance that walking under the influence of such spirits keeps a person blind, spiritually dead, and bound from achieving real success. But what's more intriguing is the fact that most believers seem to be oblivious to such truths. Jesus certainly paid the price for our freedom, but true freedom is not just the result of the sacrificial work of Jesus. It is in knowing that truth, staying mindful of it, and taking steps to apply it that keeps a person truly free.

Jesus Himself made that exceptionally clear. While He was teaching about the kingdom of God, many of the Jews who were listening believed in Him. Realizing that, He warned them about how to be free truly. "Then said Jesus to those Jews which believed on him, 'If ye continue in my word, then are ye my disciples; indeed, and ye shall know the truth, and the truth shall make you free'" (John 8:31–32 KJV). Yes, Jesus did His part. Now we must do our part by continually studying and meditating on His Word and applying it to the various situations we encounter or suffer. Jesus has broken the chains of spiritual slavery for us. He demolished the prison doors, but the prisoners must realize that fact and walk out of prison. We must step out of the prison cells from which Jesus liberated us.

Many experiments have been done to show how, when an animal or a person has been bound for an extended time and afterward released, they still act as one who is still in captivity. That's how it is for most Christians. Although Jesus freed us by His sacrificial work, the full realization of our total deliverance hasn't dawned on us. Because of that, we are still going about as if we are still bound to the evil ancestral foundations.

Moses is an example of a person who was the victim of an ancestral curse. He missed entering the Promised Land because of an inherited curse. Every time there was a seeming lack of food, water, or something, the Israelites complained, nagging at Moses and driving him to utter frustration. The Bible refers to Moses as a man who was meek and full of patience. However, there was a spiritual strongman at work in his lineage. Exodus 2 tells us that the mother and father of Moses both were of the house of Levi, meaning that they were from the ancestry line of Levi. You might ask, "So what? What is the connection?" Well, before Jacob, the father of the twelve tribes of Israel, died, he prophesied on the lives of his boys. He told them what their future would turn out. Some of these prophecies contained both blessings and curses.

In Genesis 49, Jacob called his boys to gather together. He then began to tell them their future. After pronouncing his blessing, along with some negative aspects, to Reuben, his firstborn, Jacob turned to Simeon and Levi and declared that they were instruments of cruelty. For that reason, he said, "Cursed be their anger, for it was fierce; and their wrath, for it was cruel: I will divide them in Jacob and scatter them in Israel" (Genesis 49:7 KJV). It was at least three generations previous when Jacob made that declaration. Years later, Moses, the great man of God, could not enter the Promised Land because his anger had caused him to get frustrated with the people's grumbling, so he acted contrary to the command of God.

The Israelites were complaining about not having water to drink. God gave Moses instructions to go to the rock and *speak* to the rock, saying that water would then come out of the stone. But the people were very annoying with their complaints, and they frustrated Moses. They incited his anger to the boiling point. Instead of speaking to the rock, Moses, in his anger, told the people, "Listen, you rebels. If it's the water you want, I will give you water." Moses lifted his hand and, with the rod, struck the rock twice, causing water to gush out for the people to drink. But God was not pleased with Moses's action.

What's the lesson? The eye-opening object lesson is that walking with God does not automatically immunize you from the effects of certain curses or spirits. Our immunity comes from the repenting of our sins and our ancestors', meditating on God's Word, walking according to His precepts, and engaging in biblical spiritual warfare. Peter admonished believers to resist the devil (1 Peter 5:9). Paul urged us to put on the whole armor of God (Ephesians 6:11). It is by these principles that we will benefit from the sacrificial work of Jesus upon the cross of Calvary.

For that reason, Paul prayed this spiritually eye-opening prayer for the Ephesians, for the Colossians, and for all believers:

> That the God of our Lord Jesus Christ, the
> Father of glory, may give unto you the spirit
> of wisdom and revelation in the knowledge

of him: the eyes of your understanding being enlightened; that ye may know what tis the hope of his calling, and what the riches of the glory of his inheritance in the saints and what is the exceeding greatness of his power to us-ward who believe, according to the working of his mighty power, which he wrought in Christ, when he raised him from the dead, and set him at his own right hand in the heavenly places, far above all principality, and power, and might, and dominion, and every name that is named, not only in this world, but also in that which is to come. (Ephesians 1:17–21 KJV).

THE ANGER FACTOR

I've had my share of anger. Anger had dominated my life for a very long time. After our guardian dropped us, children, off at our relative's house, I became somewhat of a rebellious child in a way I had never experienced before. It seemed like I was always in conflict. Years after having come to the United States, I was playing with a toy on the dining room floor at my mother's triplex unit. As I was playing, trying to put the toy together, I was getting frustrated. I noticed in my peripheral vision that my frustration amused my mother. When I saw that she was watching and smiling, I felt compelled to intensify the acting out of my frustration. But to her, it was funny.

The intensity of my anger started to cause angry explosions when I began to hold meaningful and steady relationships. From the very first relationship and moving on to all the rest of them, I ended up acting, saying certain things, and doing certain things in specific ways that caused friction, which incited more anger in me. Various factors sparked conflicts, for example, money issues, misunderstandings, and being forced to act in ways or do things that went against my conviction. There were times when I broke glass tables, turned over furniture, and broke household items, which I would have to replace afterward. I also came to understand that others treated me the way they did because of the specific negative energy I projected around them and toward them. Naturally, I got the returns of my projections.

Anger is not bad in and of itself. God made us with this capability to use it when appropriate and at the proper intensity. According to the American Psychological Association (APA), "the instinctive, natural way to express anger is to respond aggressively. Anger is a natural, adaptive response to threats; it inspires powerful, often aggressive feelings and behaviors, which allow us to fight and to defend ourselves when we are attacked. A certain amount of anger, therefore, is necessary to our survival."[6]

The apostle Paul exhorts Christians to be angry but says they should not sin. Don't give place to the devil to operate in and through you when the feelings of anger seem to be whirling up in you (Ephesians 4:26). We see the origin of this concept in God's dealing with Cain, the firstborn of Adam and Eve. Both Cain and his little brother offered sacrifices to God. But God chose Abel's offering above Cain's. Cain got angry. "Yahweh said to Cain, 'Why are you angry? Why has the expression of your face fallen? If you do well, won't it be lifted up? If you don't do well, sin crouches at the door. Its desire is for you, but you are to rule over it.' Cain said to Abel, his brother, 'Let's go into the field.' While they were in the field, Cain rose up against Abel, his brother, and killed him" (Genesis 4:6–8 WEB).

Anger had dominated my life for a long time. It was in my blood. Even after I had become a Christian, I was still struggling with anger. Eventually, the Lord gave me victory over this dangerous emotion. Thus, I am continually growing in grace and wisdom and take longer to become angry.

Steven Beebe, Susan Beebe, and Mark Redmon, authors of *Interpersonal Communication*, assert that one of the strategies a person should apply to control anger is to "seek to understand why you are angry and emotional. Understanding what's behind your anger can help you manage it. Realize that it is normal and natural to be angry. It's a feeling everyone experiences. You need not feel guilty about it. Anger is often expressed as a defense when you feel violated or when you are fearful of losing something important to you."[7] It took a reasonable amount of time for me to understand this fact. Anger is not bad in and of itself. Instead, it is a matter of knowing when to express it and how much anger to allow yourself to feel.

Motivational speakers and life coaches advise that a person should use the energy of his or her anger to fuel his or her passion for success and productivity.

THE NIGHTCLUB
EXPERIENCE

At age sixteen, I stumbled upon the nightclub scene, which led me to a career as a DJ at the club. It was past midnight when I left work at the fast-food restaurant and caught the bus home. Somewhat like in the *Twilight Zone*, when I got off the bus at my stop, I entered the "nightclub zone." That's one way to express it. That bus stop led to one of the main turning points of my life. As I stepped off the bus, I noticed a group of people standing around at the north end of a little plaza where the store that I'd bought chips, soda, and cookies since my early teen years was located. But I'd never noticed this hangout spot on that corner before.

Adorned with my burgundy-colored work uniform, smelling like hamburger and fries, I made my way toward the crowd of people who stood in front of the club. They were talking, smoking, drinking, and laughing. They seemed to be having a great time. Somewhat like the woman with the issue of blood in the Bible, I slid my way through the crowd until I made it to the entrance. I looked around at the people who were sitting, standing, and dancing. The DJ was playing Caribbean-style party music—reggae, soca, and calypso—along with hip-hop, love songs, and more. I made my way to the DJ booth. It was on the corner, elevated about two feet. I stood by the cabin for a few minutes, admiring how the DJ selected and shuffled the music to keep the people dancing and enjoying themselves on the dance floor. The DJ noticed my curiosity, so he kindly invited me to come up to the booth. That was thrilling.

After I'd been in the booth awhile, watching the DJ selecting and mixing the records, and enjoying the view of the people dancing on the dance floor, he asked me to stand in for him as he took a short break. He promptly showed me how to put on the next record and where to make the musical selections. It was like discovering my destiny that night. When the night was over, and it was time to leave at about four o'clock in the morning, I went home. My spirit was ecstatic. I couldn't wait to go back the next night.

The truth is, I've always had a passion for music, parties, and DJ'ing. So, the next night I returned to the club for my training with the DJ. Seeing that I was a quick learner, he started to take longer breaks to allow me to develop my DJ skills. In general, the job of the DJ in a nightclub is to play songs that are interesting enough to incite the people to get on the dance floor and keep them there as long as possible. If the dance floor empties, the DJ has to do whatever necessary to get the people back to the dance floor. While I had a fun time serving as DJ, at the same time, I felt pressured, something that motivates a DJ to hone his skills.

The club became my new hanging-out spot. It was like finding a family I didn't know I had. Soon I started to go to the club in the daytime as they were open during the day to serve food. They served Caribbean dishes such as curried goat, jerk chicken, rice and peas, and soup, among other various island meals. During the daytime, the owners and I were able to connect on a more personal level thanks to the lower-intensity, quieter atmosphere. After observing that I'd been consistent in backing up the DJ, they decided to open the club on Sunday nights for parties. And since the DJ handled Friday and Saturday nights, they asked me to be the DJ on Sunday nights. Hence, I was grateful to the DJ for inviting me into the DJ booth that night, allowing me to observe him at work, and then training me in selecting the right songs to keep the people fascinated.

To turn the page to a new chapter, the owners ended up buying a large property located on the main road where hundreds or thousands of drivers passed through each day from both the east and west directions. The building used to be a video arcade. The owners didn't waste time in remodeling the place, designing it, and setting it up according to their specifications. Once it was ready for business, people came from all walks of life to have a great time at the club.

The original DJ did not feel very much at home at the new place. Consequently, he did not stay at the new location for long. Once he left, I became the primary DJ. Other DJs came along afterward and started to cover Thursday and Sunday nights, while I worked on Friday and Saturday nights.

Presently, as a minister of the gospel of Jesus Christ, I depend on the Holy Spirit and His anointing for powerful ministering. But it was a different story altogether at the nightclub. I depended on rum and Coke, Guinness stout, beer, cigarettes, and marijuana to keep me inspired and motivated. When I was done working at the end of the night, I usually ended up at a woman's house.

DIVINE PROTECTION ON NEW YEAR'S EVE

As I look back on my life, I see how the Lord was with me and protecting me even when I did not know Him. This incredible incident happened one New Year's Eve. It was one of the busiest and most crowded nights I had experienced since I'd begun frequenting the club. I got very drunk that night; there is no other way to explain it. It was nothing short of a miracle. It was an accident waiting to happen. But God, even though I did not yet know Him and I was not serving Him, still preserved my life.

Every corner of the club was filled to the brim. I started the evening with my usual couple of glasses of rum and Coke. Then I drank a few bottles of Guinness stout. Then I had a beer or two. As I selected songs and kept the long-playing mixes going throughout the night, I kept on drinking and smoking cigarettes.

The people stayed, partying till sunrise. But I left around four in the morning. On my way out, I stopped by the men's room. That itself was also a phenomenon. I'd never seen so many guys just hanging out in the restroom before. They were smoking weed (marijuana), so I took a few puffs on my way out of the restroom. Excitement, right? Drinking all kinds of alcoholic beverages throughout the night and then topping it off with marijuana. What a mix.

It was when I got to the car that I realized my state. I was giving a few people a ride home. What made it worse, none of them had a driver's license. As I pulled out of the parking lot, my eyes became crooked. My right eye was looking toward the left, and my left eye was looking toward the right. I tried my best to straighten them but to no avail. I ended up driving in that condition, dropping the people off at their respective locations, and made it home myself. Was I that sober to drive so well that morning, or was it the protective hands of God that kept me for such a time as this?

Someone might protest, "How could you say God was preserving you when you were doing all those bad things?" The fact is, I didn't know Jesus, but Jesus knew me. The apostle Paul affirms that God chose us, not when we accepted Jesus, not when we started going to church, but "He chose us in [Christ] before the foundation of the world" (Ephesians 1:4 WEB).

There is no logical explanation as to why my car didn't crash the morning of that New Year's Day, except to say that God had mercy on me. He knows our hearts and the plans He has for each one of us; for that reason, accidents, gunshots, drunkenness, and adverse situations are not able to destroy a person before his or her time on earth is up.

TRACKING THE
PURSUIT OF GOD

In retrospect, I can see how God used various circumstances and people in pursuing me and seeking to draw my attention to His love and grace, which we have in His Son Jesus Christ. Sin was very natural for me. I tried to have my way and lead my life as I pleased; for that reason, I could not recognize what God was doing in my life. Eventually, with God's persistence and patience, I finally came to accept Jesus as the Son of God, who died and was resurrected for my sin and all humanity.

BEING CORNERED BY GOD'S AGENTS

In the early 1990s, I was hosting a couple of radio shows that played secular party music. I was broadcasting to the Haitian Creole community on one station and the Caribbean English community on the other station.

The Creole program aired Sunday from midnight to six o'clock in the morning, and the English program aired on Wednesday from 1:00 a.m. to 2:00 a.m., reaching the Caribbean community—Jamaicans, Bahamians, and so on.

During that particular season, a Christian radio program aired right before my shows on both stations. A Haitian missionary preceded my show on Sunday nights. While I was waiting and sometimes making my preparations to go on air, some of these Christian brothers tried their best to persuade me to leave my old life and to turn to Jesus.

One evening as I was about to start my show, one of the men called me on the phone as if he felt led and was on a hot mission that night to nail me down for Jesus. When I picked up the phone, he candidly asked me, "When are you going to give your life to Jesus?"

"Give my life to Jesus?" I mused. Then I quickly responded in a respectful yet defensive manner, saying, "I'm not doing anything wrong; I'm just playing good music to entertain the people. Therefore, there is no need to come to Jesus." It wasn't that I was against Jesus. I didn't know much about Jesus, although I had a sense of the fear of God.

Even though I was sincere with my reply, saying that I was not doing anything wrong, in my vintage leather bag in

42

which I kept my commercial cartridges was a bottle of beer and my marijuana supplies. These items were necessary for inspiration and motivation, or so I thought. That was Sunday night with the Haitian brothers, whom God used to try to get my attention unsuccessfully.

The other program that catered to the English Caribbean listeners on Wednesday morning (1:00 a.m.) before my show also had Christian programming. On this particular radio show, I played reggae music mostly. As it was with the Haitian missionary team, so it was at that radio station. What distinguished the two was that, instead of Haitian missionaries, at this station, it was Jamaican ministers. While I waited in the lobby before going on air, it was an older woman minster whom God put to the task of persuading me to turn my life to Jesus. I listened to her respectfully, but I had the same mindset as I'd had with the brothers: *I'm just having a great time, helping people to enjoy some good music.* Hence, I didn't see a need for Jesus.

To a real evangelist, I was a prime target. The way I dressed, and the smell of beer, cigarettes, and marijuana about me, attracted soul-seekers, faithful gospel preachers. I never had dreadlocks, but many people who knew me back then, and some with whom I interact presently, are sure that I had dreadlocks. Most times, my attire was an unbuttoned jacket with no shirt underneath. I bought a *Miami Vice* suit at least once a month. I could have received Jesus very early in life, but my blinders were hooked on so tight, I just couldn't see all that God was doing to bring me through.

THE LIGHT OF GOD SEEN BY
THE VOODOO PRIEST

I got home one evening after making my rounds in the streets. Surprisingly, there was a spiritual ceremony going on in the house. Seeing and hearing what was going on in the kitchen, I first went to my room. The makeup of the house was such that the family room, living room, dining room, and kitchen all lined up from the entrance of the house to the kitchen toward the back, and all the four bedrooms lined up adjacent to these sections as mentioned earlier. My room was the first room on the right from the entrance of the house.

Although I was ignorant about the Scriptures, I still felt a sense of the fear of God. Therefore, because of that sense of fear, I went into my room and prayed the way I knew to pray. I told God that "I don't know whether this voodoo ceremony going on in the kitchen is of You, but I'm going there.

After praying to God, I went to the kitchen area, where I noticed an abundance of food well-decorated on the long dining table. There were fruits, cakes, and other delicacies. That beautiful décor of sweets was set to honor and to call upon the spirits. Apart from the table of good, there were lots of singing and chanting going on as people circled the table in a single file while rejoicing. So, I naively joined them by taking an empty water gallon and began to beat it like a drum to help carry the chanting along. I was there just for the fun of it. I did not have the complete knowledge of the purpose of the ceremony.

At the end of the evening's ceremony, the voodoo priest began to speak or prophesy to each person who came and stood before him. When it was my turn, I stood before him as he gazed at me. He looked me over from head to toe and made two statements regarding my life. His first statement was made to my parent, as if he'd seen the light of God shining on my forehead was, "He's not an ordinary person." According to what he saw radiating from me, I would not be an ordinary person. The next thing was an instruction he gave, the purpose of which was to bring me luck in acquiring money. He told my mother to bathe me with meat and lemons and then tie them in a bag and throw the bag in an intersection on the street. For whatever reason, my parent did not bother following through with the instruction, for which I was glad. For all I know, just out of respect for her, although I was an adult, if she had requested me to do it, I would have submitted and allowed her to do it.

THE VISION, THE GIFT, AND THE VISITATION

THE VISION

One night I dreamed that I was sitting in the back seat of a car. The car was going down a road, where I saw buildings that indicated we were in England. While passing by a massive structure that appeared to be a big Catholic or Orthodox church, I saw a big sign on the top front of the building reading, "Bishop." After we passed that building, we arrived at a facility at the end of the road on the left. That was when I noticed who was driving. It was an older Caucasian gentleman with an older woman on the passenger seat, who, I believe, was his wife. When we got out of the car, they opened a wooden gate through which we entered. Inside was a serene lake and beautiful green grass. That reminded me of Psalm 23, where David exclaims, "The Lord is my shepherd; I shall not want. He maketh me to lie down in green pastures: he leadeth me beside the still waters. He restoreth my soul: he leadeth me in the paths of righteousness for his name's sake" (Psalm 23:1–3 KJV). I felt that I was literally by the quiet waters and the green grass in my dream. It was a delightful scenery.

Afterward, I noticed the couple had gone through another door and left me there alone. At that time, I also left and went out of the gate. At the time when I had that dream, I was working for a well-respected professional radio program in the Haitian community. It broadcast six hours a day, five days a week, Monday through Friday. I was their board operator, opening the show daily beginning in 1992. I'd had radio programs previously where I bought airtime at radio stations to do my private show. But this program was different in that it was my first time working with a professional group of men and women doing radio.

When I got to the radio station the next day after the dream, I asked a couple of gentlemen who were at the station if they knew what the word *bishop* meant. The first one, who was my former colleague at the station, the on-site manager for the radio program, said that he did not know what it meant. Then I asked some of the others, but nobody in that circle knew what the meaning of *bishop* was. So, I left that inquiry alone and went about my business, not concerning myself with it anymore.

It is not surprising that those men didn't know the meaning of the word *bishop* since none of us were religious people at that time. And although that term is widespread today, back then, it was not so common. I'm pretty sure that my dream was one of the various messages God was using in His pursuit to grab my attention to recognize the gift of salvation He wanted me to receive. But the meaning was yet to be revealed to me.

Some people don't think God still speaks through dreams and visions. They believe that He did that only in exceptional circumstances and that the practice ended with the New Testament. If God does not speak through dreams and visions any longer, then what do we do with all the dreams we are dreaming? Undoubtedly, many of our dreams have great significance in our lives. On the Day of Pentecost, Peter stood to correct the people who thought the disciples were drunk. He said, "But this is that which was spoken by the prophet Joel; And it shall come to pass in the last days, saith God, I will pour out of my Spirit upon all flesh; and your sons and your daughters shall prophesy, and your young men shall see visions, and your old men shall dream dreams" (Acts 2:16–17 KJV).

Author and prophetic minister Jane Hamon writes, "We are now living in a day in which God is pouring out His Spirit upon men and women of all nations in new measures. We have seen a greater release of God's prophetic voice, both through His prophets and His prophetically gifted people, than has ever been seen before. With this fresh anointing has come an increase of other manifestations of the Holy Spirit, such as the dreaming of dreams and the seeing of visions."[8]

An Answer to My Pursuit

As I was reflecting the other day, it dawned on me that God's pursuing me also had something to do with a response to some of the unspoken inner longings I had. One day as I stopped by the club when nothing much was happening, I sat at the corner of the bar on a stool. After looking around, I went into deep reflection. My sigh was, *I'm almost sure that life has more to offer than this.* I believe the Lord saw me and heard my plea for living.

When that thought came to mind the other day, I began to search. I asked the Holy Spirit to help me remember other clear instances when I was unknowingly seeking for God. Then I remembered that there was a time when I sought counsel from psychic readers.

It was very subtle and surprising how this psychic reader had gotten me to begin to take counsel from her and her team. I was speaking with someone on the pay phone, and this woman, having waited until I was done, said to me, "Even though you're laughing, you're not happy on the inside." After I'd heard that, she gained my attention. That day I decided to go for a consultation. I started to count on their counsel for my life's decisions. Since I never had anybody who seemed to care about how I felt or who wanted to give me any guidance, I began to view these psychics as my counselors. I did not know Jesus then. I was not involved with the church or anyone from church. Seemingly, deep down in my heart, I was seeking God. The Lord saw my heart just like He saw the soul of Saul, who was persecuting the Christians. He knew that Saul had good intentions, so He gave Saul a supernatural encounter and did what was necessary to draw his attention for his own sake. So it was with me. Although I was lost in sin and doing all types of bad things, the Lord saw my deep-rooted plea for help and came to my rescue.

I was exclusively focusing on God's pursuing me and was not mindful that my heart subtly was crying out to its Creator for help. Effectively, I now realized that not only did God have a plan for me since before the foundation of the world, but also that plan included His responding to the call of my heart, my inner cry for help. And that He did. He came to my rescue and saved me.

ROLAND F. ST. GERARD (BRORO)

A Gift from God through the Storm

In August 1992, a storm was forming out in the Atlantic Ocean. As this storm traveled toward the Bahamas, it continued to intensify, quickly becoming a category four hurricane. Before hitting the Florida panhandle, it became a category five. Once it hit Florida, many lives were lost. The storm destroyed a lot of houses. Many people from around the country and from the local communities responded quickly in bringing help for the victims. They brought items like clothes, hygiene products, food, and books. To help the victims, the president of the radio program, where I worked, who also had various offices of another business spread across Florida, contributed to the cause. Coincidently, one of the offices was in Homestead, Florida. Being a community leader, this CEO and the corporate staff decided to make a public announcement to invite the community to come to Homestead to volunteer. While the radio employees didn't need to go to Homestead, I nonetheless felt the urge to volunteer. It was through this volunteering opportunity that I received a great gift from God, which was a significant catalyst in helping me see the light of God.

When I told a couple of friends of mine about going down to Homestead to volunteer, they also showed interest in going. One of those friends drove his company cargo truck.

The other friend was instrumental in that he gave me some helpful insights concerning the beautiful gift I had gotten from God.

My friends and I stopped by a famous Haitian restaurant, whose owners wanted to go to Florida City to feed some people with freshly cooked food, while we were going to Homestead. After loading the truck with rice, chicken, legumes, and fried plantains, we headed south to Homestead, riding in the cargo truck, while the restaurant's owners followed in their car. When we got to Homestead, they dropped me off and continued farther south to Florida City.

When I arrived at the office location, the volunteer coordinator explained to me my assignment. I was to collect the many donated items that were piled up in one particular office unit and walk outside, down to two office units, to organize the items by category. As I was working, I felt so much joy as if I were going to receive a million dollars. As I was transferring the items from one office unit to another, I came across a French Christian book that I tucked away for later viewing. As I continued working, I soon came across a beautiful leather-bound *Ryrie Study Bible*. Although I was not yet a Christian, I felt as if I had discovered a goldmine. I enthusiastically put that Bible aside as well.

When my friends came back for me in the evening, I excitedly jumped in the truck and eagerly showed them the Bible. When the friend who was not driving saw the Bible, he too got excited about it. While flipping the pages, he mentioned to us something I didn't know beforehand, which was that he had attended Bible school. With that knowledge, he was able to show me how to use the cross-references in the margins of the Bible, where I could find related passages in different books of the Bible for expanded knowledge of a particular verse. That insight would later prove incredibly helpful as it guided me in my daily reading of the Bible.

Forging Time for the Bible

It's no joke: God was relentless in pursuing me. He used everything possible to grab my attention. It seemed that from one thing to another, He was actively creating or using circumstances or existing events to accomplish His goal of getting me to recognize Him as the Source of my salvation. Because I was spiritually blind, God had to be very patient before I would finally realize His love for me. That is why He ultimately had to send His angel to seal the deal.

One day I decided to visit my friend, who was an architect. The time was about six in the evening when I got to his house. After I'd greeted him and his wife, we talked while he was working on some architectural blueprints. I drank a couple of bottles of Guinness stout and hung out for a couple of hours. After leaving his house, I had another God encounter. This time, it was not a preacher or a pastor; it was a police officer. As I headed south after leaving my friend's home, a couple of blocks away, I approached a four-way stop sign. It so happened that a police vehicle and my car reached the stop sign at the same time. The police car was heading west, and I was heading south. Being courteous, I suggested to the officer that he cross the intersection first. As luck would have it, he was more gracious than I, so he signaled that I should go first. Who am I to argue with a police officer?

After I crossed the intersection going south, and he passed going west, he suddenly stopped. He backed up his car and turned on his colorful lights and siren to grab my attention. And that he got. The first thing I did when he stopped me was to put my hands outside the car so that he would be at ease, assured that my hands would not be reaching for any weapons.

When he got to my vehicle, the first thing he asked was, "Is your license suspended?"

My answer was, "I don't know, sir," although I knew my driver's license had been suspended.

Then he went on to ask for my driver's license and registration. After taking those items from me, he stayed in his car for a long time, reviewing my personal information. After what seemed an eternity, he finally stepped out of his car, called me over, and gave me about three tickets for a broken taillight and for driving with a suspended license.

What was nothing short of a miracle was that after giving me the tickets, the officer kept my driver's license and told me to leave. He told me I could get in my car with my suspended driver's license still in his hand and "drive" back home. It was apparent that God was at work. By this time, I'd gotten used to the movement of God in my life, although I still hadn't acquired the full revelation of who Jesus was and what I needed to do. I had not received Jesus in my life as yet, but God was pursuing to get me there. With these three infractions, there was more than enough evidence to arrest me and have me sitting in jail overnight. Since it was God at work, the officer let me go.

I made up my mind that day not to drive anymore without having a driver's license. However, I was always driving around, so I thought that taking a ride to the store, which was four blocks away, couldn't hurt. However, God was closing in on me. He had a purpose for the predicament; for that reason, each time I attempted to drive to the store, a police car would drive by. I reasoned with myself that it must be God signaling for me not to drive at all, even if it was only half a block away. Consequently, after a couple of attempts to drive to the store and getting the God signals, I stopped driving and began to depend on my colleague from the radio station to pick me up for work and to drop me back home from the radio station. He was such a blessing in that he picked me up just about every day enthusiastically.

At that time, I became restricted about how much I could go up and down the streets as I was accustomed to doing when I was legal to drive. Now, I could not drive when and where I wanted to any longer because my driver's license was taken away. Consequently, I became a homebody. I had recognized that it was God's plan, after all! I had to adapt to a new daytime routine. For the better part of the day, I read the Bible. As I kept reading the Bible day and night, a transformation was taking place in my heart and mind without my knowing it. It was like a low-burning ember in my heart, a flame that kept growing with every turn of the Bible's pages—like a caterpillar transforming into a butterfly.

Daily reading of the Bible affects a person's heart, mind, and countenance. A good friend of mine, a reggae music producer, realized the change that was transpiring in me. When he noticed that my way of talking was changing, that I was talking God-talk, and that there was a certain glow radiating from me, he suggested that I watch the local Christian television channel. From the time he told me about the Christian programming station, I started watching it as much as I was reading the Bible.

Every dose of God's Word in my heart infused me with God's presence, power, and purpose. I was becoming a kingdom-minded individual. But I still did not have a full understanding of the transformational process I was going through. I was just going along for the ride. Watching the different ministers on the television, I noticed that most of them usually did not end their programs without leading the audience to pray the salvation prayer. I also pray with them. Even then, I did not have the sense of being saved yet. It was not until the Lord sent His messenger from heaven to make an oral proclamation to me, announcing a verse of scripture, that my eyes were opened to the saving grace of the Lord Jesus. Nonetheless, because of His relentless love, He continued the pursuit. Paul affirms the faithfulness of God in pursuing people for their salvation when he said the Philippians, "Being confident of this very thing, that he who hath begun a good work in you will perform it until the day of Jesus Christ" (Phil. 1:6, KJV).

THE ANGELIC VISITATION

Angelic activities have been around ages before humans ever existed. But, not everybody believes in the existence of angels. Some folks think that angels were active on the earth once upon a time. Some people believe they were around in the Old Testament before Jesus' day, but all that ended after the close of the Old Testament era. Others suppose angels were active during the New Testament period and ended with the Bible characters. Luke writes of an angel setting Peter free from prison: "Peter, therefore, was kept in prison: but prayer was made without ceasing of the church unto God for him. And when Herod would have brought him forth, the same night Peter was sleeping between two soldiers, bound with two chains: and the keepers before the door kept the prison. And, behold, the angel of the Lord came upon him, and a light shined in the prison: and he smote Peter on the side, and raised him up, saying, Arise up quickly. And his chains fell off from his hands" (Acts 12:5–7 KJV). We read about angelic activities in the New Testament, but I have not come across a passage of scripture that indicates the cessation of angelic activities on the earth. On the contrary, the Bible talks about angels from Genesis to Revelation. And most of the prophecies written in the book of Revelation have not yet been fulfilled.

Unfortunately, some people believe in angels to the extreme. These individuals believe to the point of worshiping angels. God prohibits praying to angels. The Bible establishes that we pray to God the Father, in the name of Jesus Christ, and by the power of the Holy Spirit. When we follow this biblical format, God releases His angels to do what is necessary to deliver His children, protect them, or provide for them. We see an example in Revelation 19. While the elders, the four living creatures, and all the angels were worshipping and praising Father God, John was being instructed and shown future events that are yet to come. John got so overwhelmed by this great spiritual revelation, with his front-row seat in the throne room of God and his firsthand knowledge of an event yet to take place, far in the future, that he bowed down to worship the angel. But the angel quickly corrected John. Revelation 19:9–10 from the King James Version states: "And he saith unto me, Write, Blessed are they which are called unto the marriage supper of the Lamb. And he saith unto me, these are the true sayings of God. And I fell at his feet to worship him. And he said unto me, See thou do it not: I am thy fellow servant, and of thy brethren that have the testimony of Jesus: worship God: for the testimony of Jesus is the spirit of prophecy."

One of the original archangels who used to serve God in heaven became God's archenemy. Acting out of pride, he tried to lure glory away from God and bring it to himself. He was cast out of heaven as a result, and a third of the angels went with him.

Not only did this, used-to-be archangel drew many angels away with him to rule over them, but his grand plan was to take God's position and sit on the throne of heaven. Isaiah writes, "How art thou fallen from heaven, O Lucifer, son of the morning! How you art thou cut down to the ground, which didst weakened the nations! For thou hast said in thine heart: 'I will ascend into heaven, I will exalt my throne above the stars of God; I will also sit on the mount of the congregation on the farthest sides of the north; I will ascend above the heights of the clouds, I will be like the Most High.' Yet you shall be brought down to Sheol, to the lowest depths of the pit" (Isaiah 14:12–15 KJV).

Are angels still active today? According to Terry Law, founder, and president of World Compassion, angels are active on the earth presently. He writes:

> A story from World War I involving angels known as "The Angels of Mons" was told throughout England within a month after the battle.

Near Mons, France, in August 1914, heavily outnumbered British troops had fought with no respite for days. They had lost many men and guns, and defeat looked inevitable.

Captain Cecil W. Hayward was there and tells how suddenly, in the midst of a gun battle, firing on both sides stopped. To their astonishment, the British troops saw "four or five wonderful beings, much bigger than men," between themselves and the Germans. These "men" were bareheaded, wore white robes, and seemed to float rather than stand. Their backs were to the British, and their arms and hands were outstretched toward the Germans. At that moment, the horses ridden by German cavalrymen became terrified and stampeded off in every direction.[9]

Research shows that God uses angels in many aspects of human activity. Although humans are not supposed to pray to angels, they nonetheless converse with angels when angels initiate the conversation. According to Jonathan Macy, "Angels give trustworthy guidance, but we should be aware that angelic guidance may not come through startling visions, dreams, and manifestations, but perhaps through less dramatic means. It can be the stranger with the insightful word, the loving member of your church, prompted within by angel to offer terms of keen discernment, the stirring in your heart toward a course of action, or the inspiration to tell somebody of Christ. Angels can guide wisely, and we should be alive to how God wants to communicate with us through them."[10]

My angelic visitation helped me make the most meaningful decision of my life, the decision to turn my life over to Jesus. I first found a Bible while volunteering in Homestead, Florida. Then I got my driving privileges taken away from me. I end up having to read the Bible and watch Christian television day and night. As a result of the pursuit of God in using people and various circumstances, it happened that one evening I found myself awake at three in the morning. As I rose and sat upon the bed, I noticed the form of a person standing about six feet tall at the foot of my bed. He was not glowing or shining brightly. But the moment I saw or perceived him, he quickly exclaimed this four-word phrase, "John one, verse sixteen." As I was not accustomed to having angels visiting me, or even receiving Bible verse in night nor day visions. So, The moment I heard those words, I jumped out of bed to look in the Bible to see what John 1:16 says. Remarkably, John the Baptist, talking about Jesus, told his followers, "And of His [Christ's] fullness have we all received, and grace for grace" (John 1:16, KJV). Thus, phase one of the pursuit has After all the events, the people, and the circumstances God had utilized in His quest to bring me to the point of receiving His gift of salvation in Christ Jesus culminated that evening of October 1992.

THE DECISION

The Lord God of the universe relentlessly pursued me so that He would lead me to this point of gaining a clear understanding of saving grace. God's pursuit of me delivered me from continuing to live a frivolous and rebellious life. I have been acquitted from eternal damnation. With God's abundant grace in Christ Jesus, I am set free and have become a child of God, born anew. No longer am I paying for the offenses of Adam, I am now reaping the fruits of righteousness in Christ Jesus Jesus and reigning in life through Him. Paul makes it clear to the Romans, "For if by one man's offense death reigned by one; much more they which receive *abundance of grace* and of the gift of righteousness shall reign in life by one, Jesus Christ" (Romans 5:17 KJV, emphasis added). Thus, my bad habits did not just come from my ancestors; it was my heritage through Adam's bloodline. But now I have a new legacy in Jesus's bloodline. He is the Second Adam.

On that particular night of celestial visitation, after reading the passage the angel uttered (John 1:16), I instinctively walked about two feet away from the bed, toward the corner of the room, and knelt to pray. Like everything else throughout the pursuit process, I was being led and guided by my invisible Tutor (the Holy Spirit). As for the angel, he said nothing more than those four words: John One Verse Sixteen. And the moment I got off the bed to look in the Bible, he was out of the scene. As I was following the steps that lead to my kneeling to pray, I was no longer mindful of the heavenly visitor. At that point, I was hooked on what God was endeavoring to do. After kneeling, I stayed on my knees for a lengthy time, praying.

I don't recall all that was said in the prayer. However, God must have conveyed a vital message, instruction, or command to my spirit. My response I remember answering back to the Lord was that "In this case, tomorrow when I return to the radio station to work, I will have to tell the guys that if they still would like me to work for them, I can only play gospel music from now on." That was my response to God. There it is. It took months, if not years, for God's relentless pursuit of me to consummate. Many years ago, when I stood in the parking lot of the nightclub enjoying the Compas music exuberating from the little church across the street, I had settled in my mind that the Christians were in their world and me in mine. I did not know Jesus back then. But now I do. I now recognize Jesus to be the Son of God, who came to this earth to suffer, die, and be resurrected to pay the debt of all humanity. Because of Jesus' sacrifice, I have been set free from all my past bondages, and now embrace my total spiritual freedom in Christ Jesus.

In His pursuit of me, God used various people, events, and circumstances to guide me like a harness on a horse's face. After responded to the Lord while on my knees in prayer, I got up a brand-new person. The Bible affirms that "If anyone is in Christ, he is a new creation. The old things have passed away. Behold, all things have become new" (2 Cor. 5:17, WEB). When the Haitian missionary brothers had invited me to give my life to Jesus, I didn't see the need to do. I felt that I was where I was supposed to be, living the lifestyle I was living. If it were not for God's patience, His relentless love, and the use of His human servants, circumstances, and His angels, I would have still be lost in darkness and away from knowing the love of God.

I now have the privilege of calling Jesus Christ, my Savior, and my Lord. I came to know by reading the Bible, divinely given to me by God, that Jesus suffered and died for you and me. God raised Him from the dead by the power of the Holy Spirit, and He ascended on high, now sitting at the right hand of His Father. The Bible says that Christ is in heaven, interceding for those who put their trust in Him. He is advocating near the throne of His Father for you and me as the adversary is continuously accusing us before God day and night. But since Jesus bled profusely to save us from the wrath of God to come, He is qualified to present His blood in the courtroom of heaven on our behalf. The author of the book of Hebrews writes, "Seeing then that we have a great High Priest who has passed through the heavens, Jesus, the Son of God, let us hold fast our confession. For we do not have a High Priest who cannot sympathize with our weaknesses but was in all points tempted as we are, yet without sin. Let us, therefore, come boldly to the throne of grace, that we may obtain mercy and find grace to help in time of need" (Hebrews 4:14–16 KJV).

Public Confession of My Faith in Jesus

Although the decision to follow Christ was made privately on that visitation night, the Lord was not through with the process. Believing in Jesus and deciding to follow Him is the first step. But a public confession had to follow. I had to announce to the world that I am no longer a slave to sin but have become a child of Almighty God. Unbeknownst to me, the way the Lord arranged for me to make this public confession was by using a newly found acquaintance of mine. He was a popular Haitian musician and singer, who had recently started going to church. He used to come by the radio station where I worked and was very enthusiastic about inviting me to visit his church. Just about one week before I made the big decision, I had declined an invitation. But the next after I had decided to follow Jesus, I suddenly had a blazing desire to go to church. Hence, I did not waste any time looking for him to take to his church.

The first week, he took me to the Haitian church that he was attending. I was encouraged to be in the service. The next thing that made me feel that I would become a member of that church is that a group from the church paid me a home visit the same week. The group sang hymns, prayed, and welcomed me to the family.

However, since the Lord was still in control of the process, the following Sunday, after I started my gospel radio show at another station, my Haitian musician friend picked me up after the show to take me to church. But this time, instead of the Haitian congregation, he took me to a different church, an American church, one that was more vibrant and more advanced in appearance and technology. The worship service was energetic, and the preaching was inspiring. I was fascinated by the whole experience. I looked around, admiring the beautiful decor, the beautiful flowers, and the TV screens, and wondered how I could help make the Haitian church as attractive as the American church setting.

The next step of the process, as the Lord arranged steps, was the making of my public confession. After the pastor preached, he made an altar call. He invites people who would like to receive Jesus Christ as their Savior to go upfront before the altar. My colleague got up to go to the front; I quickly got up also and followed right after him. As we stood before the altar, the bishop had everyone repeat the salvation prayer. The person who prays this prayer publicly acknowledges that he or she is a sinner and in need of a savior, repents of all sins, and puts his or her trust in Jesus Christ, who paid the price on Calvary's cross to redeem our souls for God.

After the bishop prayed for us, he sent us to a private room with prayer counselors to advise us on how to pray in other tongues. In so doing, they counseled us on how to initiate the prayer in tongues and release ourselves to the influence of the Holy Spirit. After the praying session, they informed us that there would be a baptism the following week. Even though I was not that familiar with the Haitian pastor of the church to which my colleague had taken me the previous Sunday, somehow, I felt the need to seek his advice about whether or not I should get baptized the following week with the other church. While he did not counsel against the idea, he did explain to me how they go about baptizing members at his church and mission. To receive baptism under that ministry, one has to go through a three-month-long baptism class. After completing the baptismal class, every candidate may then receive baptism on the appointed day. For some reason, I had already felt some allegiance to the pastor and the Haitian church. For that reason, I decided to submit to his customary way of ministry operation. I waited, went through the class, and eventually got baptized by the pastor.

NEW CREATURE IN CHRIST

Can you imagine that? The God of the universe pursues people for their good and God's ultimate purpose. Paul told the Ephesians, "For we are His workmanship, created in Christ Jesus unto good works, which God prepared before that we would walk in them" (Ephesians 2:10 WEB). God will go to all lengths to redeem a lost sinner. Jesus spoke of the parable of the lost sheep, in which the shepherd has one hundred sheep with one having gone astray. He leaves the ninety-nine to look for the one lost sheep. And when he finds it, he rejoices (see Matthew 18:12–14). Peter tells us, "The Lord is not slack concerning his promise, as some men count slackness; but is longsuffering to us-ward, not willing that any should perish, but that all should come to repentance" (2 Peter 3:9 KJV). God is not looking to see how many people He can send to hell. Due to sin, we are on our way to hell, but God has made a way through His Son, Jesus Christ, to escape eternal damnation. Paul further urged Timothy to pray for everybody and for all who occupy a position of authority. He explained that "This is good and acceptable in the sight of God our Savior, who desires all men to be saved and come unto the knowledge of the truth" (1 Timothy 2:3–4, KJV).

The Lord God made us to worship and to serve Him. He desires that we please Him in the ways we live, think, and act. The book of Hebrews states, "By faith, Enoch was translated that he should not see death; and was not found, because God had translated him: for before his translation he had this testimony, that he pleased God" (Hebrews 11:5 KJV). Enoch pleased God so well that God let him stay on earth no longer. He took him without Enoch's having to go through the dying process. It was not that I pleased God but that God, for His divine purpose, chose to pursue me until He cornered me, until my spiritual eyes were able to see, and until I was able to answer His call for me to follow Him. Thus, I am no longer lost and blind but am a new creature, alive in Christ.

I give glory to God's holy name for His relentless pursuit of a sinner like me. I am no longer a slave to sin and unrighteousness. I am now a child of God forever, reborn by the Spirit of God and going through continuous heart transformation by the Word and the Spirit of God.

The love of God is incredible. He patiently and faithfully pursues people until they can see the glorious light. God took me from living a life of drunkenness, cigarette and marijuana smoking, and promiscuity, and allowed me to be one of His children and a minister of the gospel of peace.

My past is evidence of a fallen and broken man. My present is evidence of God's restoring grace. There is nothing that will ever separate me from the love of God. "There is therefore now no condemnation to them which are in Christ Jesus, who walk not after the flesh, but after the Spirit" (Romans 8:1 KJV).

What God has done for me by relentlessly pursuing me for my salvation was not because of any merit on my part. It is all grace, that is, grace upon grace. It's only God's mercy at work. I'm pretty sure He has been pursuing you for a long time. Like me, it is possible that you also have been oblivious to the pursuit of God to save you. Your desires, passions, and ambitions for fame and fortune might be factors keeping you from seeing Jesus for who He is. God went to great lengths to get me to read His Word day and night so that my heart would spark and be ready to hear and see Him for myself. Personal encounters with God are not rocket science experience. He is accessible to everyone regardless of background or experience. I pray that the Lord would open your spiritual eyes today? And that you would ask Jesus to come into your heart and be Lord of your life. You might not feel or see anything extraordinary at first, but rest assured, if you call Him with all your heart, He will not let you be ashamed. He will come to you and make His home in you.

What can you do to prepare your heart for the Holy Spirit to work in you? You can begin by taking time daily to read the Bible. As you read, also pray and ask God to help you understand what you are reading. The Holy Spirit will do the needed work in your heart, and you will begin to see Him, feel Him, and hear His voice.

As you take time to meditate on the Word of God day and night, your faith will begin to rise to the point of believing in Jesus Christ for who He is. The apostle Paul told the Christians in Rome, "That if thou shalt confess with thy mouth the Lord Jesus, and shalt believe in thine heart that God hath raised him from the dead, thou shalt be saved. For with the heart, man believeth unto righteousness; and with the mouth, confession is made unto salvation" (Romans 10:9–10 KJV). Believing in your heart and confessing with your mouth the lordship of Jesus is the key to receiving

Jesus in your life. You believe in your heart, and you declare it with your mouth.

Although God went to such extremes to grab my attention and get me to read the Bible, He is now using my story to prayerfully grab your attention and let you know that you are unique and that He has a special calling and mission for your life. When you decide to turn your life over to Him through His Son Jesus Christ, then the significance of your life will become more apparent.

Here's to eternal life!

ENDNOTES

[1] Howard B. Moss, "The Impact of Alcohol on Society," *Social Work in Public Health* 28, no. 3/4: 175–77, https://doi.org/10.1080/19371918.2013.758987.

[2] World Health Organization, "Governments Confront Drunken Violence," *Bulletin of the World Health Organization* 88, no. 9. (September 2010): 641–716, https://www.who.int/bulletin/volumes/88/9/10-010910/en/.

[3] Mayo Clinic Staff, "Nicotine Dependence," https://www.mayoclinic.org/diseases-conditions/nicotine-dependence/symptoms-causes/syc-20351584?p=1.

[4] CDC, "Marijuana and Public Health," February 27, 2018, https://www.cdc.gov/marijuana/health-effects.html.

[5] D. K. Olukoya, *Prayer Rain* (Lagos, Nigeria: MFM Ministries, 1999), 62.

6   American Psychological Association, "Controlling Your Anger Before It Controls You," 2005, https://www.apa.org/topics/anger/control.

7   Steven A. Beebe, Susan J. Beebe, and Mark V. Redmond, *Interpersonal Communication: Relating to Others* (Upper Saddle River, NJ: Pearson, 2014).

8   Jane Hamon, *Dreams and Visions: Understanding Your Dreams and How God Can Use Them to Speak to You Today* (Raleigh, NC: Regal, 2000), 18.

9   Terry Law, *The Truth about Angels* (Lake Mary, FL: Charisma House, 2006), 24.

10 Jonathan Macy, *In the Shadow of His Wings: The Pastoral Ministry of Angels—Yesterday, Today, and for Heaven* (Cambridge: Lutterworth, 2011), 111–27.

BIBLIOGRAPHY

American Psychological Association. "Controlling Your Anger Before It Controls You," 2005. https://www.apa.org/topics/anger/control. Accessed March 7, 2020.

Beebe, Steven A., Susan J. Beebe, and Mark V. Redmond. *Interpersonal Communication: Relating to Others.* Upper Saddle River, NJ: Pearson, 2014.

CDC. "Marijuana and Public Health," February 27, 2018. https://www.cdc.gov/marijuana/health-effects.html.

Collins, Gary R. *Christian Counseling: A Comprehensive Guide.* 3rd ed. Nashville, TN: Thomas Nelson, 2007.

———. *The Biblical Basis of Christian Counseling for People Helpers: Relating the Basic Teachings of Scripture to People's Problems.* Colorado Springs: NavPress, 2001.

Elfers, John, and Patty Hlava. "The Lived Experience of Gratitude." *Journal of Humanistic Psychology* 54, no. 4 (2014): 434–55.

Evans, Tony. *Victory in Spiritual Warfare: Outfitting Yourself for the Battle.* Eugene, OR: Harvest House, 2011.

Hamon, Jane. *Dreams and Visions: Understanding Your Dreams and How God Can Use Them to Speak to You Today.* Raleigh, NC: Regal, 2000.

Law, Terry. *The Truth about Angels.* Lake Mary, FL: Charisma House, 2006.

Macy, Jonathan. *In the Shadow of His Wings: The Pastoral Ministry of Angels—Yesterday, Today, and for Heaven.* Cambridge: Lutterworth, 2011.

Madugba, Mosy U. *Prayer Power: Explore the Limitless Power of Prayer.* Port Harcourt, Nigeria: Spiritual Life Outreach, 2009.

Mayo Clinic Staff. "Nicotine Dependence." Accessed June 18, 2020. https://www.mayoclinic.org/diseases-conditions/nicotine-dependence/symptoms-causes/syc-20351584?p=1.

Moss, Howard B. "The Impact of Alcohol on Society." *Social Work in Public Health* 28, no. 3/4: 175–77. https://doi.or g/10.1080/19371918.2013.758987.

Munroe, Myles. *Rediscovering the Kingdom: Ancient Hope for Our 21st Century World*. Shippensburg: Destiny Image, 2004.

Olukoya, D. K. *Prayer Rain*. Lagos, Nigeria: MFM Ministries, 1999.

World Health Organization. "Governments Confront Drunken Violence." *Bulletin of the World Health Organization* 88, no. 9 (September 2010): 641–716.